To Barbara £1

With best wishes

from Davis.

(Pages 50 - 53)

GW00372776

COLLECTED POEMS
1997

ARTHUR H. STOCKWELL LTD.
Elms Court   Ilfracombe   Devon
Established 1898

*British Library Catcloguing-in-Publication Data.
A catalogue record for this book is available
from the British Library.*

ISBN 0 7223 3042-1

*Printed in Great Britain by
Arthur H. Stockwell Ltd.
Elms Court   Ilfracombe
Devon*

Contributions are not placed in order of merit

CHERISHED GIFT

The child within does never forget
and you were the first couple I ever met,
you've always shown your love and care,
that's why I bought the teddy bears.

The word *'love'* means so much to me
and I will always cherish it as you can see,
so I was taught the cherished gift I found
and that is why I am still around.

You will never change the way I feel
in the knowledge that my love maybe,
because when you already have the best . . . .
which Jo now knows and she can rest.

With my physical strength, courage and willpower too,
and in my thoughts were always you,
with Richard always by my side
you'll all be cherished all the time.

Things are looking up so bright
it gives me enormous joy of delight.
You are also a happy, loving couple too,
and my cherished gift was found by you.

Jo

WHAT WE'VE BEEN THROUGH

I've always dreamed of fortune,
And fame, and love as well;
The first and second I'll never have,
But of the last I'll tell.
Love is a gift so precious,
Not to be thrown away,
To a person who wants nothing
But to steal your heart's bouquet.
Lovers usually end up wed,
Well, that is what is told,
And the happiest moment of your life
Is receiving that band of gold.

Now I know your body inside out
And you know mine the same;
I bore for you a baby boy,
Our love fought back the pain.
Through hell and waters high we've come,
Together, as one we've been,
And now a baby girl brings joy
To our family — our team.
We've continued up in places
Where most others would fall down;
What we've been through together,
Would make any family proud.

K. Woods

MEMORIES

We look back down Memory Lane
From a very early age,
When we could first remember
Our very first school days.

We learnt to spell and read and write,
And remember what we were taught;
Even at an early age, we had memories
To help us learn at school, right from wrong.

There are happy memories,
Also very sad ones too;
But with God's help and guidance,
We are sure to pull through.

There is a lot taken from us in life,
But one thing is there to stay,
The treasured memories of happy times
We shared along the way.

Memories are a special gift
Sent from God above,
They're always there to remind you
Of the ones you lost and loved.

When you lose the ones you loved,
There is only one thing left for you,
To hang on to loving memories
And treasure them always too.

Gracie Lawson

CANDLE

After the spark of life
the flame blossoms out
small at first, but it grows,
casting light on everyone close
darkening the shadows further out.

Problem winds blow
the flame struggles and shakes,
yet feeds off each trial
becoming only stronger.

But,
on reaching adulthood,
the wax decays away, until the tiring flame,
strong as it once was,
reflects,
yearns,
before the last wisp of smoke rises
and life is extinguished.
Forever.

Lee Mitchell

NATURE'S NOON

The sunlight glinting on the waves,
The ripples rustling on the shore,
The seagulls flying in the air
Calling for more.

The reeds all whispering in the wind
Caress the warm and dewy air.
And all the world's at peace again
My love is there.

What says the streamlet dancing on?
What intonation in his tune?
How does he know that love is here
This time of June?

The blackbird singing in the bush,
The thrush on top of yonder tree
Are but a little orchestra
To Love and me.

All yellow grows apace the wheat,
All statuesque the golden corn.
In shady corners poppies grow
Where love is born.

In village and in town we stray
Admiring garden, house and home.
We'll live at home ourselves some day
All on our own.

Thomas W. Splitt

THE LONELY PATH

Up in the kind of place where
No one dwells, the hills stretch for
Miles without interruption. Only the
Sheep know these hills well and
Make their way across them by a
Lonely path which seems to lead from
Nowhere to nowhere. I sometimes tread
This lonely path alone, almost losing
Myself in desolation where no
Other living person can be found.
For miles the path stretches
Over hill and dale, over brook
And stream and seems to meander
Aimlessly, seemingly going nowhere.
But I do not worry, as the
Air is fresh, my legs are strong
And I make good speed along the
Path as there is nothing to hinder
Or intervene.

Thomas W. Splitt

THE SEA

Only water, spume and foam
Dashing along your outer edges,
Dashed by the unseen, the wind,
Yet driving schooners, barques and caiques
To unknown destinations.
Wet, yet dry with salt,
As the stories that are told,
As the stories unspun,
As the fables recounted and yarns unfolded.
On a sunny summer's day as you lap
In restless movement at my feet
As I sit on a concrete jetty,
Dabbling my toes in gentle wavelets,
I long to plunge in your waters cool,
And dive to depths in crystal waters clear,
Watching squid and shrimp and eel
Floating about to feed and dive and swim.
But not now, not when you crash with force
Against the pier and wetten everyone in yards
With spray, ceaselessly battering the promenade
And lifting ton stones and rocks,
Sending them hurling in the air.
Faithless friend, at once so sweet,
Only to finish up as a rogue,
A brutal, antagonistic force of death.
Do not keep me from my darling,
Do not make us stay apart,
But be kind and loving, and let me sail
Across the narrow strait in between.

Thomas W. Splitt

THE RAPIDS

They carve a way
Down through the gully.
What torrents have flowed
In ages past
To have cut out such
A deep embouchure?

We paddle in a little pool
At the edge,
Or sip a taste of
Snow-cooled water.
We even dare take our canoes
Down the cataract.

Beside what nice clear crystal stream
Must I meet my Love?
In what pleasant shady glade
Shall I romance?
Not beside this terribly
Turbulent water.

Love swims in yonder limpid pool
And stands and drips all over me.
The passions I feel are not like
This little rill.
They plunge onwards and downwards
Like the torrent!

Thomas W. Splitt

THE VISITATION

Love has passed on now nearly five
Years ago and has left me wondering what
I am to do on my own. I visit the
Church where we were wed and memories
Flood back to me like a gentle shower.
I spend hours alone in the half-dark and
Although I am not superstitious I can
Sometimes feel her near. That is until one
Evening towards midnight the curtains swished
Even although the windows were closed. The
Dog growled even although it was sound asleep.
The door creaked even although there was
No wind and I could almost swear a
Faint shadow passed between me and
The light. I could only suppose it was love who
Was coming to see if I was alright. My
Heart beat, my body froze, but I felt no
Fear as the apparition soon disappeared.

Thomas W. Splitt

THE RAINBOW GATE

The rainbow arches across the sky like a
Great bow. I pass through the rainbow gate into
A vastly different world, a world of fairies,
Pixies, gnomes and elves, of fairy princes and
Princesses where nobody grows old, the
Flowers never die and the sun shines
All day. I have entered this fairy realm where
I can be at peace, where I eat ambrosia
Till I am satisfied and feast on all sorts of
Delights in this blessed world. But the time comes
When I have to leave, bid farewell to my
Fairy friends because the rainbow is dying and
I have to get back to my mundane world and
My daily toil. But how the fairy world has
Cheered me up, a touch of Shangri-la and
Whetted my appetite for diviner things.

Thomas W. Splitt

SUFFER THE CHILDREN

I have spent the day with my great-grandchild;
Is she ever meek; is she always mild?
The playful scamp has captured my old heart!
In her life, which will play the greater part —
Wilfulness which is set in her nature;
Or the goodness which is there to nurture?
But, wilful or meek,
Each child is unique —
To guide, do we seek?
Give hope to the weak?
Children by two parents are begotten;
Can parental duties be forgotten?
When the cement of character is mixed
And the foundation of behaviour is fixed,
Neglect by parents cannot be pardoned —
As base for future is set and hardened.
The formative years;
With laughter and tears;
The gaucheness and fears,
As puberty nears.
Not solely a child can be a truant;
Missed — a parent — and guidance pursuant
To impose discipline whilst it is taught
That, within the child, good control is sought.
All else above, nature, nurture are lost
Without love, wisely shown, not heeding cost.
Parents to be there
To show loving care;
To discipline, dare;
In all to be fair.

By loneliness, ridicule or rancour;
Left in life's rough seas without an 'anchor';
In many ways men and women abuse,
Yet only physical torment is news!
For, guidance by example is a must,
As children grow and learn in loving trust.
Trust, a winning ace
With home a firm base.
Gives hope as they face
The world in life's race.
There are many hurdles with which to cope;
Hard to tackle without the skills and hope.
Parents and teachers, worthy of their salt,
In turn need to face teenagers' revolt
With understanding until symptoms cease;
It is curable, as a child's disease.
Growing stage by stage,
Support at each age;
In trust to engage
Tensions to assuage.
A treasure, not a trophy to display;
A young life, not a plaything to mislay;
No commercial asset to make a gain;
The wish to grow in love never in vain!
A child, an advert for the parents' nous;
A model for goodness others can view.
A living treasure,
Born to give pleasure;
Worth without measure
At school or leisure.
Child exploitation known through the years,
And, alas, today abuse still appears.

To deplore the hype for self-promotion,
Does not prevent the rightful emotion
Over each sad case which is recounted
Where abuse against a child is mounted.
Agencies beware
Abuse, here, is rare;
Child is in best care
With own parents there.
Agencies are prone to over-react;
In dealing with parents show lack of tact.
The ways of children make mock of guidelines;
Love and commonsense put codes to sidelines;
And with them put the debate on smacking,
Control only wrong when love is lacking.
There is no set rule,
And no magic tool;
Just show love and you'll
Not be proved a fool.
Parents, with loving control, your way steer;
So, as their trust grows, you will one day hear
Each child say, as fears become redundant,
'I've come so that you have life abundant'.
Succour the children for all that is worth,
For, by such will come the kingdom on earth.
'Suffer the little children
'To come unto me;
'And forbid them not,
'For of such is the Kingdom of Heaven'.

Roy Hammond

B

WHY CREATION?

My human brain, it cannot comprehend
The vastness of space — without any end!
Did God really plan it — sun, moon and stars;
Each galaxy and planet; Jupiter and Mars?
Was there a 'big bang' — a huge explosion —
Before angels sang, man was a notion?
What eternal purpose did such action cloak;
The thought does occur, God was having a joke!
It must have been God's plan — surely not a stumer —
Showing when He made man a sense of humour!
Genesis fable; the Darwin theory;
Choose if you're able; all makes me weary.
Was man on this earth,
The cause of God's mirth?
Then did man's lack of troth
Lead to Biblical wrath?
Can you envisage
'In His own image'?
It would seem the experiment ended;
To other worlds it was not extended!
Intelligent life — has it yet been found?
Seemingly not rife, universe around.
Can it really be — in all creation —
Only you and me bear a relation

To the Creator, and so it would seem
Can be in touch with One who is supreme!
Is it a treasure?
Does it add pressure?
It causes great grief,
Men state in belief
They're doing God's will
When they fight to kill!
So, while some in their simple faith nestle,
With thought of the cosmos many wrestle.
A cosmos so vast — talk of a 'black hole' —
And man has been cast in a leading role?
Is he still in favour, despite all his weakness?
Does he have a Saviour, supreme in His meekness?
It seems all beyond my understanding;
Why creation? — and in it man's standing?
And yet, through the haze
A thought to amaze —
He who reigns above
Is as thrilled with love
As a maiden found
Here on worldly ground!
For, as I search for a cosmical clue
An overwhelming love keeps breaking through.

Roy Hammond

DEVIL'S ADVOCATE

Lent certainly activates the mind;
I find
Myself posing — what do I believe?
For how long do I grieve?
Or is it time to rejoice?
I presume that is His voice!
Amidst life's noise, can I hear what He has to say?
Is any of it relevant to this day?
Throughout life we've learned the story,
And how it ended up in glory — glory!
The human brain cannot conceive it.
Redemption — do I truly seek to receive it?
God born on earth as a man;
Is that how it all began?
Without a human father —
Stretches credibility even farther!
Incarnation —
To achieve man's salvation;
Does that seem
Rather extreme?
Jesus as truly God
As on this earth He trod;
Then how can a man He fully be;

Just as weak as you and me?
The events of Holy Week He foresaw;
Yet, God's cause He foreswore?
No! — that way He rejected;
To humiliation and pain was subjected.
Can I, with my human brain,
Assess His suffering and pain?
What did He feel?
In worldly terms — was it real?
The third day —
Absurd say
Many who rely on their intellect.
I struggle my thoughts to collect;
I do not understand;
Yet, on the other hand,
So full is my heart,
I cannot start
To accept it is all a lie;
For then, love and hope would surely die!
When my heart rules over mind,
I find
Love and hope where'er I go.
Why? — I simply don't know.

Roy Hammond

I DON'T BELIEVE IT!
The Church of England publishes another report

The Church now reports that there is no Hell!

Tell me, from what were we saved by the Cross?

Because, if our sin does not sound the knell,

What becomes of my faith? I'm at a loss!

Take the central tenet of salvation —

Of belief, are we to discard the core?

For if the Bishops throw out damnation

There will be no need for Christ any more!

Roy Hammond

DO — RATHER THAN DON'T

Yes, I've shown impatience and been curt;
But never meant to be rough;
Never purposely set out to hurt —
Now, I ask — 'is that enough?'

For have I ever swallowed my pride?
Turned to show the other cheek?
Thought carefully before I've replied?
Been counted among the meek?

Have I ever set out to be kind,
Quietly without a fuss?
To serve those who are weak or maligned,
By myself, anonymous?

Have I held the hand of one in need,
In privacy of the night?
So giving of myself without heed,
Like the widow and her mite?

'I have never done anyone harm',
Although good to a degree,
Is lesser than reaching out an arm —
I must heed the Lord's decree!

Roy Hammond

"JESUS WEPT"

It never is blasphemy
When I say "Jesus wept";
A meaning it has for me,
As that night Peter slept!

Jesus shed tears as He gazed at that fair city,
Over desecration and sinfulness therein;
And He wept again and showed Martha great pity,
As He saved Lazarus from the grave and from sin.

Does not Jesus weep today
O'er abuse on this earth?
And for all, does He not pray —
For spiritual rebirth?

On watch in Gethsemane Peter fell asleep,
Forsaking Jesus in His hour of watchful prayer.
Later, in his guilt, Peter, we are told, did weep;
His denial of Christ proving too hard to bear.

Oh! have I the vigil kept;
Been faithful to my creed?
In repentance, have I wept?
Made aware of my need!

Jesus lives today amidst our weakness and pain;
Shut out the worldly clamour and you'll hear Him weep.
Yet comes the call to repent and to live again;
Be watchful and pray and His promise He will keep.

Luke 19.41; John 11.35; Matthew 26.40, 26.75

Roy Hammond

NOT FOR SALE

A closing-down sale!
Let me set out my stall —
It ought not to fail,
With gifts for one and all.
All that I display
Has been freely given;
An offer today —
The truth by love leaven.

Yes — there is no cost,
Just accept with good grace;
For you are not lost,
If the truth you can face.
'Love was dead', you thought;
Swiftly comes the reply —
'It's free — can't be bought;
There's an endless supply.'

You don't need my stall,
Just go straight to the source;
And give Him a call;
Faith will show you the course.
I'm feeling so tired,
And I need a long rest;
With hope I am fired —
For ever I'll be blest.

Roy Hammond

ONE LAST LOOK BACK

Paris on a golden morning
Long before rush hour is born,
Paris tranquil on an empty road
Bathed in the misty heat of morn.

This last feel of foreign land
Heading for reality,
Was it just a dream of golden fields
Of crickets singing, or banality?

Did we wander by quiet stream
And among foreign tongues take wine?
Did we wander golden lanes
And under moonlit skies did dine?

One last look before we go
To busy port and ferry,
Teeming people heading homeward
Back to jobs and ties and worry.

Eunice Doyle

EMPTY IS

Empty is how I feel.
Worried is how I look.
Scared is how I am.

Life was simple once,
Why can't it be again?
Always feeling the need, to worry so much.

Bad times seem to come so often,
I try to shut myself off,
Pretending everything is fine.

We should be taught "life is never easy",
No one ever prepares us for the shocks in life.
The simplest things are there to trip us up, why?

Me, I'd welcome a life that wasn't difficult,
Embrace it with open arms.
So for now I'll live on in my empty lifeless life.

Ruth Alderson

MY GARDEN

A little bit of Eden, my garden is to me,
A quiet calm oasis, complete with apple tree,
A paradise where I can be totally content,
For I know this patch of soil is truly Heaven sent.

Secluded is my garden, and I can feel quite free
To close my eyes and thank my God for giving it to me,
For He is here beside me, I feel His presence near,
I merely have to whisper, and know that He will hear,
Faithfully providing creations daily fare,
Spreading us a banquet, showing tender care.

Roses bloom around me, everywhere I gaze
Bees and butterflies abound, in midsummers haze,
How sweet the sound of birdsong early in the morning,
The chorus rings from every tree just as the day is dawning.

Perfumed honeysuckle drips with morning dew,
I'm so glad it's summertime, I love it so don't you,?
Surrounded in my garden with so many lovely things,
I feel so close to Heaven that my cares have taken wings.

When by trials I am pressed,
My garden is a place of rest
I trust that you will pardon this long soliloquy,
But this is how I feel and what my garden means to me.

Mary G. Kane

ALL IN A SEASON

This winter'll be a mean one
Set aside from the ones of past,
All but in the will of remembrance
Give the next a chance.

Autumn the cue for nature to ramble
Illusions created by colour,
Trickery and teasing
Bramble living its fullest.

Wildlife putting their lives on hold
If only to be able to sleep.
The flesh and blood behind closed doors
Springtime air a cause for applause.

Sally Craddock

UNSURE

When alone I start to think,
I think so hard my feelings sink;
I fill with panic and feel unsure
And hope one day my mind will mature.

I need direction in my life,
My miniature stress and hopeless strife.
Others have more worries than I,
Yet when alone I still cry.

I want help but no-one hears,
My heart is full of people's fears;
I long for salvation in my dreams,
But in reality, there are only unsure pleas.

Heidi E. Sowter

THE SIREN

The song of the siren
Wails in the distance.
And yet, even now when it is heard
Backs shiver, eyes dart
And all minds thinking the same —
'Please let it pass'.
For a moment, just a brief moment
We are all the same.
Children listening, imitating the high tuneless pitch.
The young harshly reminded of their own mortality.
Parents grouping together in thoughts of pity,
And the old feeling it's all too familiar.
The rich and poor
All races, all ages
For a moment look at each other differently.
All secretly scared together
Until the siren stops screaming.
Then we all go on as before,
Blind to one another
Ignoring each other but
With our ears still ringing with
The song of the siren.

Sharon E. Boulton

AT WORSHIP

A PRAYER FOR TODAY

Lord help me on this sacred day —
And guide me as I bow to pray;
O may I hear Your deep clear voice,
Lord make it now my only choice.

Dear Father God, I know You're here,
Lord let me feel Your presence near,
For then I'll know that I am thine —
And Your great love is truly mine.

O come into our meeting Lord,
May those who've gathered hear Your Word —
And if some here don't understand —
Lord in Your love take hold their hand.

Lord clear the mind of each one here —
So they can hear You bright and clear;
May Your grace and power be known —
To each who're praying on their own.

Thank You dear Lord on this Your day,
And for Your help, whilst we now pray;
Guide each one here, Lord bless each soul,
God cleanse us all, with Heavenly coal.

Then as we go into our world —
And when the flag of Christ's unfurled,
May Your power be strong and clear —
Proclaiming that Your love is here.

AMEN.

oooOOOooo

17th November — 1996   *John W. Hopkins*

JUST — SOMETIMES — LORD

Sometimes the 'Light of life' seems out,
Shadows reveal the human doubt;
But, brightness intercepts the dark,
It surely will then make its mark.

Sometimes "Men" don't hear Your voice,
The mind has made another choice!
So help us Lord to listen more
And not to shut Your open door.

Lead us dear God so near to You,
We will then see Your light anew;
Lord guide us when we seem to doubt,
Dispatch Oh God, the evil bout.

Then, when the 'Light of life' seems dim,
May we pray, free us from sin;
Dear Saviour, CHRIST, we trust in You,
Oh may our thoughts, be pure and true.

And sometimes, when our thoughts seem bare,
Lord hear us then, You're surely there —
To guide us in Your blessed way,
May we be true to You each day.

Then, sometimes, when one's light seems out,
We hardly know our way about;
May *we* then see, 'The Heav'nly light' —
For that's switched on and always bright!

oooOOOooo

28th October — 1996   *John W. Hopkins*

C

THE BOUNDLESS LOVE OF GOD

The great love of our God —

                    is a wonderful thing,
For He controls one's life —

                    until His bell doth ring.
If we will just trust Him —

                    in all we think or do,
Our God is so faithful —

                    to the many or few.
It is important each day —

                    to talk fully with Him,
To read His divine Word —

                    for His light is not dim:
So, ask for His guidance —

                    when 'you' start each new day,
And listen with great care —

                    to what He has to say.
Sometimes we are unsure —

                    of the way we should go,

For we all need a guide —
>
> when our surety is low.

Have faith in our Saviour —
>
> put trust fully in Him;

His love will not waiver —
>
> But! His freedom we win.

The love of our Lord is —
>
> so powerful and strong!

He will lead us to vict'ry —
>
> whilst to Him we belong:

Through Christ Jesus our Lord —
>
> Vict'ry cometh our way,

When we Christians meet Him —
>
> in His Heaven some day.

oooOOOooo

10th September — 1996   *John W. Hopkins*

ON BEHALF OF THE YOUNG

* * * * * * * * * * *

WE THANK YOU LORD

We thank You dear Lord for guidance in life —
To help us daily avoid total strife;
For evil is strong 'midst loud earthly din,
Spreading distraction — it's hard then to win.

Sometimes it's difficult in freedom to fight,
As Satan's so strong when showing his might;
For some of the young find it hard to keep clean
When evil is there, wheresoever they've been.

Evil's attractive, e'en that which is banned;
But, Your Spirit is there just where "they" now stand,
If they will allow in freedom to see —
The trouble they are in, so "they" can be free.

We thank You dear Lord for all that You do,
To help them in life find freedom through You;
Lord, as Your Spirit's alive in our world,
I thank You and pray, great joy is unfurled.

Today! evil "men" are tempting our youth,
And "they" are so wrong and very uncouth;
We thank You dear Lord for guidance in life —
To help us direct them from Sin now so rife.

oooOOOooo

19th August — 1996   *John W. Hopkins*

IN PRAISE OF GOD

God's in His Heaven, we should be happy and free;
He is there when we need Him, e'en if it is me:
He's watching o'er His people each day throughout life,
And he can keep us all free from ungodly strife.

Love is truly a gift from our Father above,
For He makes us so happy with infinite love;
He can show us the way even when we are lost,
And His love is for ALL without quoting a cost.

Sometimes in life the way is hard and uneven —
Because we have o'erlooked our Father in Heaven;
God's always available when one's mind's in a turmoil;
Just speak with Him in secret, and listen the while.

So, how do we contact Him I hear you now ask!
I must tell you dear friend, it's not such a big task:
For He's there when we need Him, just kneel down in prayer*
You will find that God your Father, is always there.

*If you cannot kneel, just be sure God understands.
The effectual prayer of the righteous availeth much, and
He is listening to you. His blessing is available to all.*

oooOOOooo

27th July — 1996   John W. Hopkins

I AM CONTENT

I am content to do Christ's will
For Him who climbed Golgotha's Hill;
He bore the pain for you and me,
He's crucified, mankind to free:

I am content to go His way —
And talk with Him from day to day,
For He then guides and leads me on —
To pastures new and free from wrong.

I am content to read God's word,
In which it tells about our Lord —
And all about the sin of 'men'
So helping me keep free from them.

I am content when times seem tough,
E'en all my thoughts are also rough,
&
When nothing wants to go my way
God's voice unheard by me that day.

There is a lesson here dear friend —
To help us each until life's end;
It is to trust our Holy Lord
Who loves us all, we have His word.

*ARE YOU CONTENT? IF NOT — You can find comfort in
Jesus Christ. Read the Holy Bible and pray.
HE WILL ANSWER
TRUST HIM.
TODAY.*

oooOOOooo

July 16th — 1966   *John W. Hopkins*

AM I RETIRED — LORD?

Am I retired Lord, have YOU given up on me?
"They" say I'm too old, but I'm still happy and free!
I'm still able to serve You my Saviour divine,
With Your strength within me, Your grace then makes
   me fine;

You know my strength Lord, so I'll be guided by You,
And whilst I'm healthy I'll be certain so to do;
For what I so wish is to be true to 'God's Word'
Helping and acting in close accord with my Lord.

We're as old as we feel some may say about life,
When perhaps it should be, 'until God's in one's life':
For, some, though retired, may feel just lost to the world,
Yes! A gap needs filling to bring happiness untold.

And, Do you now question, just what can that gap be?
I suggest it is JESUS, Our Saviour is He;
For some are retired though they are not very old,
"They" are just tired of this life, or so I've been told!

So! Do something for Jesus, whate'er it may be,
It will surely do good and give blessing, you'll see!
For He is the fulcrum of much love in this world,
And He'll make you happy when HIS flag is unfurled.

Don't retire yet, in spirit, my dear unknown friend,
Set to work for King Jesus 'til life has to end;
And then you will meet Him when life's work is ALL DONE
Singing praise to King Jesus — HIS blessing's then won.

oooOOOooo

6th May — 1996   *John W. Hopkins*

WHERE ARE YOU LORD?

Where are You Lord, when one feels so ill;
Or when one is bored, feeling tired and still?
Where are You Lord, when sometimes in doubt?
"We" then question what life is about.

Where are You Lord, when "we" do not know
Which way to turn, so follow the flow?
Where are You Lord, when sometimes we're weak?
Our eyes seem blind, when Your love we seek.

Where are You Lord, when "we" are bowled out?
Feeling depressed, in anger we shout.
Where are You Lord, when "we" sometimes just
   cannot find peace?
"We" can only pray for God's love to release.

Hearing my plea from Heaven above, I hear Your
   voice —
With infinite love, when we often miss what's just out
   of view —
For You our Lord, help more than a few.

In HIS great love, through God's Spirit divine, pray to
   Him now —
His grace is sublime.

Where are You Lord?

You're there in the Hospice, comforting the dying;
On the street You're the Man, bad weather defying.

In the jail with the prisoner, serving time for his crime,
Yes, there with the homeless, or the one doing "time".

You're there in Hospital; the nurse or the doctor,
Comforting and healing, or just as the proctor.

You are there too my Lord, when wickedness is rife;
Destroying all good things, and happiness in life.

You're there when kind people, feed those who're so hungry,
Give blankets to warm them, and all good things sundry;

Then on the good Sabbath, the preacher's proclaiming —
The love of our Saviour, in all that he's saying.

For God is Christ's Father, the Redeemer from sin;
He's there at the behest of each one who love Him.

oooOOOooo

March 13th — 1996   *John W. Hopkins*

HIGH HOPES OF HEAVEN

I'm sure there is a place called Heaven,
And that all its cream teas are made in Devon.
If I go there I want no ration
To when I indulge in my cricket passion,
Except on the days when I plant trees,
Or visit farms sampling crumbly Cheshire cheese,
Or lie on sands by a warm, blue sea,
Or walk on lovely heights like the Hills of Clee.

I hope they serve English breakfasts there,
And that old men like me regain their lost hair.
I hope they've got some red wine fountains,
And escalators on fine lofty mountains.
I hope they play football any time,
And that you can have legs like those in your prime.
I hope they have roast joint on Sundays,
And, as in my childhood, cold meat on Mondays.

I hope they have endless cups of tea,
For people with an unusual thirst, like me.
I hope they have herbaceous borders,
And Chinese take-aways, for late night orders.
I wonder whether I might just dare,
On the very slim chance of me getting there,
To slip these notes in my coat pocket.
Do you think I'd get a terrible rocket?

Jack Finch

THE UNFORGETTABLE IMAGE OF ONE CHILD'S PAIN

Images may well change the course of history,
Amongst them the searing picture that sent shock waves
From Vietnam's war thundering.
Many would never in a lifetime forget it —
Alan Downes' chilling picture of the little girl,
Running naked, napalm burning.

That tragic child, with skin melting from tiny frame,
Forced shocked humankind to face barbaric weapons
Used in this most cruel of wars.
Napalm victims stay critical a month or more,
And eighty per cent of them die — most painfully.
This was no great and noble cause.

Screen images like this built up a heart-felt plea,
Worldwide, against the purpose of that deadly war.
Many called for conflict to cease.
American campuses flared into action,
The young shaking the nation's conscience, and the world's.
This led to a return to peace.

The human mind cannot absorb the blinding pain
Of tens of thousands who burned and died in one day,
From old age to childish years —
Belgrade, Coventry, Dresden, and Hiroshima.
But all of us who saw that pitiful picture
Felt one child's pain through angry tears.

Jack Finch

FLYING LIKE A WITCH

High above the tree tops
Low beneath the sky
Hanging like a rainbow
Watching like a fly

Dark as any shadow
Silent as the night
Waiting like a viper
Dancing like a kite

Watching for a moment
Taunting like a child
Lurking in the shadows
Hunting in the wild

High above the tree tops
Low beneath the sky
Hanging like a rainbow
Watching like a fly

Clare Barnard

'MRS POTS'

There was an old woman
who had many pots
Which she had bought in half-dozen lots:
Some were round
Some were square
Pots ··· she had them everywhere.

And in those pots
all ninety-two
Is where her many flowers grew:
Pink and white
Red and blue
Flowers she had of every hue.

And all her flowers
she would sell
To Miss Ivy Litchen-Dell:
Buttercups and daffodil
Hydrangea for the window-sill,
Lupins and forget-me-nots
Here ends the lay of Mrs Pots.

Ballina, N.S.W.,   *Robyn J. Gould*
Australia.

A N G E L S

Have you seen an angel recently?
Did he look just like you and me?

Or did he have a pair of shining wings,
And play on a harp with golden strings?

Did he come down to earth from the sky?
Or was he the one who didn't pass on by?
When you were desperate at your wits' end
Was he the only one who was your friend?

God has sent His angels down to earth...
To guard each of His children from birth,
Sometimes, in a form we do not recognise,
'Ordinary' people who can change our lives.

So let's take comfort each and every day...
That one of God's angels is never far away.
A stranger we entertain...to our surprise,
Could turn out to be — an angel in disguise!

. . . .

Hebrews 1:14
*"Are not all angels ministering spirits sent to serve those
who will inherit salvation?"*

Hebrews 13:2
*"Do not forget to entertain strangers, for by so doing some
people have entertained angels without knowing it."*

5th May 1996   *Sheila Ann Rowland*

LAMB   OF   GOD

"John saw Jesus coming towards him and said, 'Look, the Lamb of God, who takes away the sin of the world!'"   John 1:29

Agnus   Dei
Lamb of God
Sacrificial lamb

Agnus   Dei
Lamb of God
Saviour of sinful man

Agnus   Dei
Lamb of God
Was slain at Calvary

Agnus   Dei
Lamb of God
Died to set us free

Agnus   Dei
Lamb of God
Resurrected on high

Agnus   Dei
Lamb of God
Ruler of earth and sky

Agnus   Dei
Lamb of God
Will return again

Agnus   Dei
Lamb of God
ETERNALLY YOU REIGN.

12th December 1995   *Sheila Ann Rowland*

MORNING

Sunday morning, day of rest,
Awakened early, not at my best.
Came downstairs to wash pots and dishes,
Tidy round and feed the fishes.
Coffee on, breakfast ready,
Go sit down and watch some tele.
Sunday morning gone already.

A. D. Swindlehurst

NOT LONG TILL SUMMER

Willow trees weeping, along the lane,
All of a sudden it started to rain;
People running into each other
As they are dashing for some cover.
Raindrops bouncing off the floor
As I closed my front door;
Looking at the brochures in hand,
Dreaming of sun, sea and sand.

A. D. Swindlehurst

IN GOD'S CARE

My heart is broken
   And my body is aching,
For the hugs, and kisses
   From you it's yearning.

You've gone to the heavens
   So high above,
Where there is no evil
   Just everything good.

You'll spend your days
   In God's love and care,
And you'll always be happy
   And protected there.

My sweet little child
   You died so young,
You were taken from this world
   When your life had just begun.

J D Clark

BUSTER LLOYD-JONES .... VET AND AUTHOR

For all the sick and lonely ones,
I clasp my hands in Prayer.
Where Life, once full of promises
Became quite bleak and bare . . . .
The handicapped who cannot see,
　　　　　yet still can hear the birds,
Whilst others in their silent world
　　　　　just long to hear your words . . . .
Those talented, so much admired,
　　　　　successfully have won
The battle that was almost lost,
　　　　　because they could not run . . . .
Their courage, will and fortitude
Stands out beyond compare
With humour and a kindly word
To cheer us everywhere!

Make the best of what you have
These folk have shown the way . . . . . .
The longest mile can be worthwhile
Where hardships ruled the day!

*Buster was the Founder of DENES NATURAL
HEALTHFOODS FOR ANIMALS . . . . . . , confined to a
wheelchair for life through Polio.*

PER ARDUA AD ASTRA

D. L. Rayner-Campbell

FROM HIGHER REALMS

Although out of sight,
          I shall always be there . . . .
I am but a whisper away . . . .
Like a song that has ended,
          but still lingers on . . . .
Created forever to stay.
Although out of reach,
          I live on in your heart,
With memories that once we knew,
In peace and tranquillity,
          where time stands still
Sending echoes of Love back to you.

D. L. Rayner-Campbell

JACK WARNER

Though known as Sergeant Dixon,
In reality called Jack,
Throughout the years your fame increased
And never once looked back,
The characters you played so well . . . .
And other wartime shows . . . . .
The brilliance of the Blue Lamp shone,
As everybody knows.
That light for you will always shine,
Bright as the Evening Star
Towards the closing of the day,
Although it seems so far . . . .
We still can hear your "Evening All"
Now whispered with a sigh . . . . .
You're out of touch, not out of mind,
"Good night" is not "Goodbye".

D. L. Rayner-Campbell

RED-LETTER-DAY

The privilege of growing old
No longer gives one pleasure
When all the loved-ones have passed on,
With only thoughts to treasure . . . .
Just pause, and think of those alone
Still waiting for the post . . . .
Apart from never-ending bills,
Friendship is needed most!
It costs so little just to say
"I hope you are quite well,
And better still, for having this,
Though little news to tell."
        So give a thought to lonely folk
        And write without delay,
        A word of cheer, from far or near
        Makes one Red-Letter-Day!

D. L. Rayner-Campbell

THE VULTURES

During the mad rush
Coming and going
I failed to notice
Certain "signs"
No doubt pent up for me
In days long past.
Again it was left and right
Lone or North?
Jackie or Hillary?
Heather or Gwen?

Seeking that which cannot be found
I hurled myself through
Days and nights of evanescence
Oh my God! trying to avoid
The evil of the world wise
Those to whom death is of the other
And a source of inspiration
And creative intelligence.

So I flew away
Leaving the town
Where I was born
Seeking that which could not be found
Until, of course,
I found her.

It was her name,
You see,
The river of life from
The beginning of the book
Of life.
Making 1977 my last days.
Saint Germaine en Lay.

Having returned whence I'd come
I found things had changed considerably
And the beast was upon me
With his political party
And Hollywood friends and
Rock and roll music.
I survived for a time
Living in comfortable seclusion
Ignorant of their "reality".
Noticing those personal details
Were changed by a hand unknown
To me and not concerned in the least
That I should return.

Gradually they stole everything
Including my birth date!
Spencer Gulf, Ferguson Avenue,
Clinton Street, Howard and Hillary!
Who would have thought to recall
These persons from so long ago?

But it did not end there
Far from it
Making me lose my mind and memory,
As if all were but a dream
That "belonged" to somebody else.
Which in a sense it does
As money, time, energy and power
Tend to change things to
Rewrite history
To their own ends
Totally against my will
Desire and wishes
While Genevieve aged
And Maggie,
From those distant years,
Was "reborn"
Revitalized
Or given a new media image
Which, naturally, they call
"Privatization".

There is no future beyond the past
While tidings of truth
Are set free
So that a world may be
Impoverished
Materially
Spiritually

Morally
Simply because I failed to return.

Two girls called Elizabeth
Another called Grace
But from distant parts
Where there is no distinction made
Between right and wrong
Other than what sells
Or will they buy?
Streaking forth the years go by
To a lake in Switzerland
Where I wait for a boat to take me
To the other side
Where in just a couple of days
I'll see her
And touch her
Only because she loves me.
But ten years later
With things all gone
And media hype everywhere
It begins to drag me down
So that I may know pure evil
Rather than good.

But it's now too late.

St Peters,   *Lubo E. Ceric*
South Australia.

A WINTER'S DAY

Pale winter sunshine filtering through
The trees and branches so bare,
Birds circling high above in the blue,
There's a lifelessness everywhere.

Frost still gripping not relenting
Its hold upon the ground,
Shades of evening soon descending
Closing the day with no sound.

The moon appears, a ghostly white
High in the frosty air
Lighting the darkness of the night
For the wanderer out there.

The wise old owl sits in the tree
Staring down, watching for prey,
A moonlight night being easy to see
So he can take a rest by day.

Winter so slow in passing
With short days and cold
Seems a long time before spring
When all nature will unfold.

Dorothy Price

TO BELIEVE

Yesterday is but a memory,
Today will quickly end,
Tomorrow, it may never come
On what can we depend?

Thinking, we expect it will
Light and darkness alternate
Knowing in this existence
Of our revolving planet.

Having confidence in the truth
Of that which we believe
And also come to accept
In the things we achieve.

Knowing how much we value
The truth in everything,
The trust that's also given
Is reliable and continuing.

Faith to believe in Jesus
To realize what that means,
Jesus who gave His life
We believe, our life He redeems.

Dorothy Price

A PLACE APART

Through forest and woodland green
There flows a clear rippling stream
Making a happy little song
As it splashes merrily along.

Cool and refreshing amid the shade
Over and beyond the glade
Where dragonflies flit around,
Peace, and quietness doth abound.

It's very pleasant to linger there
Being an ideal place for prayer,
Seems a special part of creation
Where one can rest in meditation.

Sensing freedom and timelessness
With nothing at all to oppress,
Drawing nigh unto the Lord
Who is so very much adored.

Dorothy Price

PEACE AT EVENTIDE

The blackbird sweetly singing
High up there in the tree
Happy with his life so free,
Happiness also he's bringing.

To all who hear his song
As the sweet sound draws
And it bids us to pause
Just before we move along.

Taking time in the evening
When the working day is done,
Gazing toward the setting sun
With its rays still beaming.

There's a stillness and peace
At the end of the day
When the noise melts away
And all the rush doth cease.

Dorothy Price

SWEET FRAGRANCE

The concern on a gentle face
That says I understand,
With words unspoken
The friendly touch of a hand.

Like fragrance from an old garden
Drifting softly on the air,
Roses fading, past their best,
Nevertheless, perfume everywhere.

Life is like a garden
Sometimes fresh and bright,
Other times dead and lifeless
With life hidden out of sight.

But there will be a revival
When things are made anew
Living in hope each day
While looking forward too.

Following the master's footsteps
Doing as He would do,
Helping someone along the way
A worthwhile life to pursue.

Dorothy Price

OLD MEMORIES

When I grow old and very tired
   and spend my days in dreaming,
The dream I'll cherish most of all,
   the one I'll want to tarry,
Is of the girl I loved so dear;
   beyond all earthly scheming.
But who, alas I lost because,
   I took too long to marry.

I was a soldier in those days
   and served my time abroad.
I left her home to wait for me
   to finish off my time,
And spent my days in happy dreams
   of all I could afford.
A wife, a home and children there,
   in truth, a life sublime.

But, just before my time was up
   and I was due for home,
A letter came that broke my heart
   and changed my future life.
My own sweet girl had met a man
   with whom she chose to roam.
So, here am I, just dreaming
   now of how I lost a wife.

*Dedicated to a dear friend of mine
who served with me in India.*

H. R. Cullen

WHAT ARE WE TO DO

There's always a reason
                  but who understands
why man wages war
                  in faraway lands
was it jealously started
                  the blood flowing fray
or greed that is causing
                  all turmoil today
the heartache confusion
                  the tears in our eyes
so scared for our brothers
                  who fight for our lives
so proud of those people
                  they battle a cause
to stop victimisation
                  an end to all wars
but bombs don't rain freedom
                  guns don't fire hope
with cries all around me
                  prayers stick in my throat
what are we to do
                  to make all this cease
until man intermixes
                  how can there be peace.

Rosalyn Howell

MICROSCOPIC BEAUTY

The microscope with exquisite clarity
      Reveals an arcane Beauty never seen
      But through its lenses. In it sharp and clean
We see forms not elsewhere can we see
Of complicated regularity —
      Nature's arcanum. Always crystalline,
      She builds from cell to cell with art unseen
Her miracles of wrought geometry.

The lovely patterns in the microscope
      Of balanced symmetry inspire a joy
That holds within it the rich germ of hope.
      The beauty manifest has no alloy,
'Tis fundamental — Nature's inner sign
Is surely witness to a life divine.

Henry Harding Rogers

E

WARTIME

We fought to end war, young men so brave
To foreign parts sent, the country to save.
The tanks rolled by with guns ablaze,
A battle to death, in those dark days.
In the midst of this hell, there she stood
Brave and defiant, as no other could,
Dressed as a man she carried a gun
But, under all that she was like, a nun.
Time was stolen in moments odd,
In places strange, from the war's fighting mob.
There we found love in this troubled land,
The differences felt, close at hand.
Under protection from battleground,
A flower beneath dirt this beauty I found,
A woman, from lands with trouble and strife
When conflicts cease, will become my wife.
The war is now over, I am homeward bound,
I write to the sweetheart I had found,
Months to negotiate, months to arrange,
At last beside me in a land that is strange.
Time takes with it anxiety,
A new life for her here with me
In love and married, the war in the past,
Against all odds, we are happy at last.

Patricia Evans

THE SPIRIT CHILD

She left us like a yew tree
Branch blown in the sky,
Peeping her pretty toes on high.

An eiderdown of clouds,
Fleecy and warm, but eddies of snow
Floated towards the Styx below.

They were beyond the reach
Of man but nature did
The yew repair and hid.

Then Magic showed her mantle —
The bough's regeneration —
A bud was her creation.

Nola B. Small

LOVE FOR LIFE

Think of the vine that beareth the wine
think of the seed there with-in.
Think of the seed that beareth the need —
to die for life to begin.

Think of the tree, for all earth to see
think what it thinks it might see.
Think of its pride, so high it can't hide
I wonder if that could be me.

Think of the flesh when morning is fresh
think of life breathed with-in.
Think of the cost, if life shall be lost
but think of its end, to begin.

Think of the night, no vision, no sight
breathing still, not a word.
Think of a star, and beyond so far —
so still, like nothing un-heard.

But think of the morn, again once born
so colourfully nude, without shame.
It speaks without fear, without shedding of tear
think, and think on with the same.

Think of the part you play in your heart
the world as you stand on its scene.
Then think of the rest, to them do your best
think of Love, in our world, we're a team.

Michael A Massey

THE MAGIC OF SHERWOOD

The silence of the early morning
Oh! what a blessed time of day,
When all the world is sleeping
And only the birds hold sway;
A rustle of leaves in the forest
A canopy of mist o'er the trees,
Diamond dew on the mossy green paths,
And the hum of awakening bees.
Weak sunlight shines thro' the beeches
Like shafts of gold thro' the green,
For this was the forest, in days of old
Where Robin Hood was seen!
If you stand quite still and listen,
I'm sure you could hear a lute
And the happy sound of laughter,
Or the haunting strains of a flute
Was dear Robin really a noble?
Did his men really dress in green?
Was the pretty smiling Marion
In the walks of Sherwood seen?
Imagination is truly a wonderful gift
As I stand here alone in the dawn,
The silent forest, seems to come alive
With the voices of those who are gone!
Abruptly! the silence is broken,
By a startled blackbird in flight!
And while I've been dreaming, the mist has gone
And Sherwood is sunny and bright!

Marie D Taylor

THE WILD BUNCH

We rode out from the ranch before daylight,
It was the best time of the day to ride,
Before the dogs were astir — or the cowhands!
With my mare as my willing guide.

She knew where she was heading,
I relaxed and gave her the rein;
We travelled this way every morning,
Out on the lonesome plain.

We were heading for a natural great divide,
Formed by nature, long before man;
We stopped for breath, and the colts to rest,
At least that was my plan.

Then away to the left came a sound like a storm,
Disturbing the quiet air;
The old mare quivered, picked up her ears
And snickered as we waited there.

Then we heard, rather than saw them,
Their canter became a race;
Down in the ravine, without being seen,
They kept their tremendous pace.

Thundering thro' the silent canyon,
Sure footed in the semi-dark,
Wild horses! knowing every inch of the ground
In this massive natural park.

How vibrant, how sleek they were,
So full of power and grace;
Shining coats in perspiration
In this frantic morning race.

I slid from the horse beneath me,
Held the reins of the second and third;
In silence they stood — a trio,
Watching the flying herd.

We looked from the ridge
As they raced from the shadows,
Without even lessening their speed;
Carried on their race at such a wild pace,
They outran the tumbleweed.

I laid my cheek on the old mare's neck,
As I stroked her nodding head;
She whinnied soft, then turned about,
Not waiting to be led.

She stood quiet as I mounted the saddle,
Then nudged the two young ones to follow;
She had looked on their sire — one more time,
Leading his herd from the hollow.

Marie D Taylor

THE HAUNTED BALLROOM

The glow from the castle windows
Flooded the lawns with light
While orchestral sounds of music
Filled the warm summer night;
I crossed the lawn in a hurry,
Then softly trod a back stair,
The strains of a waltz filtered upwards
As magic filled the air;
I stood in a darkened doorway
Upstairs on a balcony wide,
In order to watch the splendour
Of the crowded ball, from inside.
I admired the beautiful crinolines
Of every conceivable hue,
While above their satin and laces,
Eager faces shone happiness too!
The dancing went on 'til morning,
Above were the chandeliers bright,
While on the stage, the orchestra valiant
Played on in the glittering night!
Bewitched by the sights in the ballroom,
I moved from my doorway at last,

One step forward! a sudden sneeze!
And I stood there alone aghast!
For the moonlight flooded thro' the windows
And shone on the empty floor!
While all around were layers of dust,
I'd never noticed before;
I walked in the moonlight, down the wide stair,
Trod a floor that was polished, and warm;
Sweet violin strains, filled the air,
As I stood alone in the dawn.
Then strong arms, reached out and held me,
As we twirled around in a dance,
Around and around the ballroom floor
On a night made just for romance!
Around spun the handsome soldier,
I can still feel the swirl of his kilt;
Excited, breathless and happy,
Enveloped, in the music's lilt!
But! — once more, the sneezing beset me!
Then oh! what a sorry plight!
For I was dancing alone, in an apron
In the middle of a moonlit night!

Marie D Taylor

SPIRIT OF GRACE

'I Am The Way.
Follow Me,' said Jesus.
'The Father is in me
And I in the Father.'

Worker of miracles
Through God's Holy Spirit.
Proof that the Kingdom
Of God is upon us.

'I Am The Truth.'
He volunteered suffering
To rescue his siblings.
'I Am The Life.'

OUR HOPE

Some say
There is no God.
Or why does He allow
Such evil in the world and do
Nothing. Yet our Creator knows our need
Of which the cost to Him was great.
His only Son, belov'd,
Paid this freely,
For us.

Alwyn Jolley

"SPRING"

How wet the day, how dark, no sun,
Will Winter never end, and Summer come.
There are puddles on the patio again,
Raindrops, beating on the windowpane;
Don't be impatient Summer will arrive,
And everything needs water, to survive.

Take a closer look out of your door,
So much you have not noticed before,
The Sparrows, feeding off the "Russian Vine",
Its tiny buds for them, are filled with wine;
What of "Winter Pansies" deepest blue,
Do they not mean anything to you?

Put on your mac, and take a stroll,
Around the garden, there is much to see,
The Clematis, fast climbing up a pole,
Blue Tits, building in the Holly Tree;
Everything is being newly born;
And there must be rain, to swell the corn.

Be patient man, forget the strife,
The world is filled with "Vibrance of Life";
Did you not hear the Robin sing?
Or see the Blackbird, on the wing?
I heard, and saw them both above life's din;
On this, the first, and wondrous day, of "Spring".

March 1992   *Deirdre Hayward*

"THE CRY OF A GULL"

When the sun's sinking red,
And the tide's on the ebb,
In the quick of evening's lull,
I sit on the jetty, away off shore,
And wait, for "The cry of a Gull";
Far out at sea, it comes to me,
As it has many times before.

No song, so sweet as the Robin's,
The Blackbird, Thrush, or Lark,
Only a Gull can bring you,
The cry of a lonely heart,
No escape from the gales, Winter unlocks,
Just a narrow ledge, on the face of a rock.

I patiently wait, watching the sky,
For the start of a rapturous sound,
Hundreds of Gulls, appear from the clouds,
And gently, alight on the ground.
Never they touch, never they clash,
Each bird, has room to turn round.

Though they live in a world apart,
They show no fear of man,
They come to find my car where parked,
And take fresh Spratts from my hand;
Then as one, they land on the mud,
To feed upon worms, in the sand.

As if to the clock, they rise in a flock,
The same as they do each day,
Circle the sky, then with a cry,
Fly into the clouds, and away;
God did not give them a song to sing,
Just a perfect machine, controlled by two wings.

A work of perfection, created so,
To weather the gales, with ice, and snow;
I sit on the jetty, way off the shore,
Where I have sat, many times before,
At the ebb of tide, in the evening lull,
God will send me, "The cry of the Gull".

November 1990   *Deirdre Hayward*

"SITTING ON THE STOOL"

Each morning when the clock goes "DING"!!
Mummy says to me, —
"Stay there Bear; I'm going out,
To make a cup of tea." —
I lay quite still, — and "think things"!
While I am waiting there,
I wear nice "Blue Pyjamas",
'Cause I'm a "Special Bear".

I am not yet old enough,
To go along to school,
So when I'm dressed, all comfy,
Mummy sits me "On the Stool";
I sit there very quietly,
The house is often full; — of "Visitors".
I size them up, "Sitting on the Stool".

Aunt Dorothy, comes on Thursday,
She sings quite well, I guess,
She has large feet, very thin legs,
Think, she wears a "Woollen Vest".
Most of them are very nice,
Mary is quite sweet,
Others lack that "Spice of Life",
Mum says they're indiscreet."

A lady came the other day
Accompanied by her son,
She swanked about his — "'bility"!
And the things he'd not yet done,
"Why Deirdre plays with "Teddy Bears"'!!
I really can't conceive,"!!
He gave a sniff! — no "Hankie" —
So he wiped it on his "sleeve"!!

I've a pretty handkerchief,
I'll not loan him that;
It's all safe in my pocket,
Folded nice and flat;
So I sit upon "the Stool",
There's nothing, that I miss,
One day when I go to school,
I'll tell the kids 'bout this.

1995   *Deirdre Hayward*

"BEAR GETS CAUGHT OUT"

It was Christmas in our Cottage,
We were 'cited as could be;
Mummy made it pretty,
And sat us round the tree.
We were in our Bassinet,
Some were on the floor;
Others, on the Settee,
There were "oodles" more.

Mummy dressed the Christmas Tree,
Lovely as could be,
Sparkly things, and Fairy lights,
For everyone to see.
Loads of cards arrived by post
From here and overseas.
These were all hung on the wall,
Near to Rose, and me.

A picture came from Winnipeg,
Of "Kimmy" on the piano,
With Golly, singing Xmas Carols,
Clever little fellow,
We had a super-duper time,
With lots to eat, and drink,
Then Mummy patted all our backs,
To make us "burp" I think.

Then she put us all to bed,
"Now quick, you must be,
Santa's coming late tonight,
You must not peep you see."
But we just pretended, —
And when Santa came at three,
Kimmy played the piano,
And we all danced round the tree.

Suddenly we heard big footsteps,
Coming down the stairs!
"Dekko"!! "Here comes Daddy," —
Said Rosie, looking scared;
All the bears climbed in their prams,
He-de-diddle-de-de!!
Santa scrambled up the flue,
Fast as he could be.

Kimmy hid inside the piano,
That left "only me" —
Dad said "Bear, where have you been?"
Now quick I had to be;
I shivered in my "Woollen Socks",
As he looked down at me;
Then, I thinked a great big "Whopper",
"I've only been to Wee."

December 1993   *Deirdre Hayward*

F

"APRIL IS A LADY"

"January" has been away,
  Resting, I have heard folk say;
Now she's back with us today,
  Clothed in furs, and jewels gay;
Rosy cheeks, from chill of air,
"Jack Frost", sparkling in her hair.

"February" dark, and shy,
  Does not stop, hurries by,
Dreads the feel of Ice and Snow,
  Has to come, — wants to go.
Everything here, fast asleep;
  Waiting for the sun's warm heat.

"March," that "boisterous Virago",
  Full of anger, puff, and blow;
Rushing, roaring, round and round;
  Razing buildings to the ground,
This old woman, I'll be bound;
  Should be out of sight, and sound.

"April" is a "Lady"
  Who gently, takes her place,
Beneath the "Almond Blossom" tree,
  With such "amazing Grace";
Where hundreds of pure white Snowdrops,
  Make a carpet of "finest lace".

Every month will take its turn,
  For an allocated space,
Making sure to wrap the Earth,
  In its fond embrace, —
But "April is a Lady"
  No-one, will ever take her place.

1986   *Deirdre Hayward*

"PASSING THROUGH"
"Gracie and Golly"

The paths are silent, where you used to tread,
A page is turned, another Chapter read;
For life is held, by just a "Silken Thread"
And I must face the world, without you.

The memory of your love, when things go wrong,
Will help me try to reach you with this song,
For at God's Will, a bird shall cease to fly,
A lovely Rose, must fade, and die.

Yet when I see the spot, where now you lay,
I know you're only just a "sigh away",
And when I leave this world, I'll be with you;
We are but "Travellers" passing through.
Just "Travellers" — "Passing Through".

1995   *Deirdre Hayward*

"THE GARDEN IS ASLEEP"

Come, look out of your window
On this bright, and sunny morn;
You'll see the Roses blooming,
And dew upon the lawn.
The garden in its glory,
Has a message to impart;
It tells a true "Love Story",
Bringing joy, to fill your heart.

Come, look out of your window
When evening shadows fall.
A Silver Moonbeam sheds its glow
Of light, to cover all.
Let every flower, in Peace abide;
His watch, the Lord, doth keep;
So gently close the curtains,
The Garden is Asleep.

1987   *Deirdre Hayward*

"DOWN IN THE FOREST"

Down in the forest, something stirred,
To herald the break of dawn,
Quietly, sweetly, on the air,
A new "Love Song" was born.
Down in the forest, something stirred,
More lovely, than the "Spoken Word";
Could it be magic — this sound I heard?

Nothing I saw, but a stream trickling by,
A feint ray of sun, breaking the sky,
The Dray of a Squirrel, in Elm tree high.
Here, there was freedom, here there was space —
Everything mattered; "Amazing Grace".
Down in the forest, something stirred, —
It was only the "Song of a Bird".

1995   *Deirdre Hayward*

"LITTLE BROWN LEAVES"

Where are you going "Little Brown Leaves"?
The wind has blown you off the trees,
Like clouds of Confetti everywhere;
Leaving the Elms, and Oak trees bare.
This way, that way, dance and play,
Over the hills, and far away.

You who did grace the branches, now bare,
Like delicate lace, on Parasols rare,
Shimmering and waving, high in the air,
Beauty you had, beyond compare;
Giving shade, from the sun's hot glare;
No-one could ever forget you were there.

I sat in my car, watching you play;
Where would you be, at the close of day?
Jumping, prancing, with never a care;
Round, and round, then into the air.
Paths to the right, paths to the left;
Which one would you take for the best?

Ever the wind will blow you ahead;
Over the lawn, to the garden shed;
Bigger the leaf grows, more for the bed.
Hundreds joining in the race;
Flying, landing with delicate grace;
Eager to find the cosiest place.

There you will lay, a self-composed heap;
Close to each other, then quietly sleep.
No-one will disturb you, until the Spring;
When the gardener comes to dig you in,
To the newly-made flowerbeds,
With sun and soft rain —
The "cycle of life", will begin again.

Little brown leaves, go — lay in your bed,
Huddled together, against the shed;
The wind will not blow you;
No feet there will tread;
When birds start to sing, and the sun is Red,
You'll awake, you're just sleeping, you are not dead.

Days had passed since I was that way,
The wind still blew, the trees still swayed;
But when I opened my curtains again,
There upon my windowpane; —
Was a little brown leaf —
It had lost its way.

I went outside — brought it in,
"Poor little love, where have you been?"
I did not take it to Belfair's Shed,
"It wants to live here," — the "Robin" said.
I laid it in our garden, instead,
Beneath the Pansies, on Gracie's Bed."

February 26th 1997   *Deirdre Hayward*

"SNOWFLAKES"

Gently they fall, like feathers from a "Dove",
Silently forming a blanket on the ground;
Snowflakes white from "Heaven" above;
Wrapping the earth, in a Shroud.

Trees, their boughs bedecked in white,
Move like ghosts in bright moonlight;
Sound of traffic, then is dull,
All the world, sleeps, in a lull.

Snow will sterilize the earth,
And warm the plants, till they give birth;
Sun will come 'ere long we know, —
To very gently, melt the snow.

The world will once again be green;
We'll think, — maybe it was a dream;
Yet in our hearts, will ever wake
The magic and beauty of Snowflakes.

"To Inez"

December 30th 1996   *Deirdre Hayward*

"SAM"

'Twas early Jan, snow upon the floor,
I found him waiting at my door,
Brown Suit, Red Vest, dapper little man;
"Welcome, you need breakfast, little Sam."
Two eyes like bright glass beads, looked at me,
"I'd be very glad, if you'd help her and me."

His dish was filled for him by me,
Sultanas, cake and grated cheese;
His nest was cosy, in the Holly Tree;
He brought his little brown wife, to me;
I'd call him gently by his name,
In an instant, down he came.

The bond between us, stronger grew,
He'd food and safety, — this he knew,
Yet he would not always stay,
Sometime — he would go away;
He did, — the second day in May;
Sam, and my heart, both flew away.

There's nothing now — but empty hours,
I could never bring him home,
It's not within my power,
I wait alone and quietly pray,
"Will we meet again, one Winter Day?"
We do not know; it's not for us to say.

"To Dr Sophie Tomlinson"

January 1997   *Deirdrie Hayward*

TINKERBELL
(The cat that jumped in the soup)

Tinkerbell is a lovely puss
Likes a great amount of fuss.
She goes everywhere about,
Sometimes in and sometimes out.

Here all the cats form in a group.
They will never jump in soup!
All wear collars, Oh, so bright,
You even see them in the night!

Tinker wears a collar now
To join the group she said, "Me-ow!"
An open window she jumps through
Exactly like she used to do!

When I take a walk so slow
Tinker comes as well, you know.
People laugh — are not unkind,
For Tinker walks on slow behind.

Tinkerbell is never a fool
Wherever she goes she has her own stool.
She sits on her hind legs, Tinker knows best
That is her stool when she wants a rest.

Coming to live in Maidenhead
I find her asleep upon my bed.
Getting so spoiled, feeding so well,
We all love her, our pet Tinkerbell.

Hilda Moss

DON'T BLAME THE CAT!

One day on the lawn
We saw to our sorrow
Tinker had caught
And was eating a sparrow!

"Oh, Tinker," said Garry,
"You are a sinner."
Then later we all had
Chicken for dinner!

MY GRANDMA

"Life is short, but God is good,"
She said, and liked it well.
As she was eighty-two, I thought
How can that be to tell?

She gently smiled and said to me,
"With friends and loved ones gone,
You know that life is short for you,
When all is said and done."

"Life is short, but God is good,"
She would insist was true.
Oh! Grandma, I know what you mean,
I understand it too!

My Grandma's trust in God was such
She did not worry overmuch,
With love and care, she always knew,
He, at the end, would see her through.

Hilda Moss

A PROMISE OF HEAVEN

In our hospital beds
We woke early at seven.
I looked at my friend,
She'd come back from Heaven!

She'd had such a dream,
Everywhere was so bright.
She was happier there,
It was her delight.

It was "Beautiful, beautiful,"
She repeated again.
Tears came in her eyes
As she tried to explain.

"That I went to Heaven,
Your friends will you tell?"
I promised dear Frances,
That all would be well.

Now I have heard
She has gone from here.
I pray you are happy
In Heaven my dear.

Hilda Moss

LOVE

Who really knows, where love they will find?
Staring us in the face, love can be blind.
This powerful emotion, the next being hate,
We make our choice, and leave love to fate.
Only in our heart, do we know our love is real,
If we have found love, how it makes us feel.
Thinking we have found it, but being led astray,
Love came calling, but wasn't meant to stay.
When love finally finds you, you're hit with such a force,
Heart pounding, butterflies, you're on the right course.
Don't turn love away, and what you feel inside,
So much love to give and share, shouldn't be denied.

Maria Carmen Lee

GENTLE TOUCH

Teach me what to say o Lord.
Please teach me how to pray.
Tell me of all things that are good.
Please tell me what to say.

Teach me as I go through life,
To keep away from any strife.
Please help me Lord from going wrong.
Pray keep me straight and keep me strong.

O Lord I cannot ask for much,
Just my soul, your gentle touch.
Grant for me my prayer is just,
And keep me honest is a must.

Lord tell me which way I must go,
Please take my hand if I am slow.
Show me in this world today,
The deeds to do, come what may.

Please show me how to be more humble.
Lord hold my hand, don't let me stumble.
Please show me how to be more kind.
Don't leave me please, too far behind.

February 1997   *Michael John Horswell*

CARROTS AND COURGETTES

The Jazz Cafe
is full of people a chattering.
Nice hot soup
in large speckled bowls.
Even the homeless can't starve
in this snug little place.
I counted the squares
on the red tablecloth,
instead of reading
the dull dreary newspapers.
The smooth music glided on
without a squeak
from the saxophone.
No politicians peeping out
on soapboxes here,
just mild filtered coffee
and a place full of people
in loud woollen jumpers
a chattering.

Tom Clarke

MOUNTAINS AFTER RAIN

The mountains are seen in full magnificence again,
For they seem as though washed of any hideous stain.
The water bustles on at pell-mell pace,
Hiding many an ancient scarred rock face.
The thunder of the waterfall fills the air,
And slippery and damp is each stone stair.
Away into the valley the flood of water sweeps,
As very few of its treasures now it keeps.
Cans, tins, bottles are whirled on their way,
As though pushed along by a giant at play.
The thunder of the water falling over the cascades,
Evokes a feeling that from the memory never fades.

N.S.W.,   *Bruce McWhirter, M.A.*
Australia.

THE CROSS-COUNTRY

Hark to the pounding pounding feet,
As running shoes and earth loudly meet.
Pounding, pounding along the fence,
Running, running there seems no other sense.
The body loudly whispers, now pause,
But the mind will not utter such a clause.
Press on, press on until the end you reach,
Though the body says rest and pause I beseech.
But soon the long awaited end is in sight,
The onlookers cheer the leaders with all their might.
The school cross-country is over for another year,
And the winners we all loudly cheer.

N.S.W.,   *Bruce McWhirter, M.A.*
Australia.

G

THE SWIMMING CARNIVAL

See the arms and legs flash in the light,
Threshing the water with all their might.
The champion and favourite soon surges ahead,
Almost leaving the other swimmers for dead.
The cheer squads voice encouraging cries,
Which make the swimmers' spirits swiftly rise.
The champion has now drawn well into the lead,
And victory now for him seems certain indeed.
Shortly the finishing line he gains,
Though not reached by him without any pains,
For before the victory voiced by many throats,
On his style and limb movements he made many notes.
With time and speed for ever in his ken,
He now swiftly and agilely springs from his victory pen.

N.S.W.,   *Bruce McWhirter, M.A.*
Australia.

THE WORLD'S GREATEST GIFT

At Christmas time was seen God's greatest gift,
To ailing, failing proud man.
A Baby, God's Son in the world took His place,
A Baby who one day as man would be lifted up,
So that all might look to Him,
And see the salvation that God through Him had wrought,
But only following a life of self-denial,
Lived in the humblest surroundings known,
And ended by kiss of a traitorous friend,
And a death perhaps the cruellest known.

N.S.W.,   *Bruce McWhirter, M.A.*
Australia.

CHRISTMAS DAY

Divine power and strength came down at this time,
Upon a world ailing, sorrowful and empty,
A world that had seen much of war and strife,
Poverty, disease and tyranny.
But God's power came in humble guise,
In the form of a tiny Child virgin born,
Born in the humblest place known,
A stable occupied by creatures of the field,
And in a country filled not with riches or might,
But dominated by the might of conquering Rome.
Humble shepherds were the first worshippers at the
    young king's cradle;
Then followed wise and ancient men from country far.
But now all the world worships Him on this day,
On Christmas Day the world's greatest birthday.

N.S.W.,   *Bruce McWhirter, M.A.*
Australia.

MOUNTAIN CALM

Oh heavenly mountain calm,
Which comes like healing balm.
Here troubles and cares seem far away,
Here I can enjoy the silent meditating day.
The ferns and grass grow unendingly down the rock,
As though fortified against all earthly shock.
Moisture and sunlight are the two blessings they crave,
No other substance do they need to save.
Happy are they to live out their short passive life,
Quite removed from stress, pain and strife.
Man a supposedly higher form,
Can wilt beneath the fast approaching storm,
While the moss and fern on their rocklike rest,
Suck up the falling moisture which they consider best.

N.S.W.,   *Bruce McWhirter, M.A.*
Australia.

MEMORIES

In the gardens of memory, I wander,
Down a crazy path or two,
Dreaming of you.
Rolling hills slip by,
With babbling streams anew.
Pausing on the rustic bridge, with slippery clots of moss,
Trees wave majestically, with bluebells a mass;
On swan-like stems, do lady's-smock sway.
With squirrels at play, hedgehogs are nibbling,
Where life begins anew, amidst the morning dew.

D. Jean Brent

BELIEVE

Sweet Jesus, with our Father too,
With eyes to see, the days shine bright;
Falling rain waters His golden earth.
Listen to Him, the Holy One.
Plant my seed, then I am pleased.

D. Jean Brent

INDEX TO AUTHORS

Alderson, Ruth	*27*
Barnard, Clare	*44*
Boulton, Sharon E.	*31*
Brent, D. Jean	*102*
Ceric, Lubo E.	*54-57*
Clark, J D	*49*
Clarke, Tom	*95*
Craddock, Sally	*29*
Cullen, H. R.	*63*
Doyle, Eunice	*26*
Evans, Patricia	*66*
Finch, Jack	*42,43*
Gould, Robyn J.	*45*
Hammond, Roy	*15-25*
Hayward, Deirdre	*75-89*
Hopkins, John W.	*32-41*
Horswell, Michael John	*94*
Howell, Rosalyn	*64*
Jo	*5*
Jolley, Alwyn	*74*
Kane, Mary G.	*28*
Lawson, Gracie	*7*
Lee, Maria Carmen	*93*
Massey Michael A	*68*
McWhirter, Bruce	*96-101*
Mitchell, Lee	*8*
Moss, Hilda	*90-92*

Price, Dorothy	58-62
Rayner-Campbell, D. L.	50-53
Rogers, Henry Harding	65
Rowland, Sheila Ann	46,47
Small, Nola B.	67
Sowter, Heidi E.	30
Splitt, Thomas W.	9-14
Swindlehurst, A. D.	48
Taylor, Marie D	69-73
Woods, K.	6

INDEX TO TITLES

All in a Season	29
Am I Retired — Lord?	39
Angels	46
A Place Apart	60
"April is a Lady"	82
A Promise of Heaven	92
At Worship — A Prayer for Today	32
A Winter's Day	58
"Bear Gets Caught Out"	80
Believe	102
Buster Lloyd-Jones — Vet and Author	50
Candle	8
Carrots and Courgettes	95
Cherished Gift	5
Christmas Day	100
Devil's Advocate	20
Don't Blame the Cat!	91
Do — Rather Than Don't	23
"Down in the Forest"	85
Empty Is	27
Flying like a Witch	44
From Higher Realms	51
Gentle Touch	94
High Hopes of Heaven	42
I Am Content	38
I Don't Believe It!	22
In God's Care	49

In Praise of God	37
Jack Warner	52
"Jesus Wept"	24
Just — Sometimes — Lord	33
Lamb of God	47
"Little Brown Leaves"	86
Love	93
Love for Life	68
Memories	7
Memories	102
Microscopic Beauty	65
Morning	48
Mountain Calm	101
Mountains After Rain	96
'Mrs Pots'	45
My Garden	28
My Grandma	91
Nature's Noon	9
Not For Sale	25
Not Long Till Summer	48
Old Memories	63
On Behalf of the Young	36
One Last Look Back	26
Our Hope	74
"Passing Through"	83
Peace at Eventide	61
Red-Letter-Day	53

"Sam"   89
"Sitting on the Stool"   78
"Snowflakes"   88
Spirit of Grace   74
"Spring"   75
Suffer the Children   15
Sweet Fragrance   62
The Boundless Love of God   34
The Cross-Country   97
"The Cry of a Gull"   76
"The Garden is Asleep"   84
The Haunted Ballroom   72
The Lonely Path   10
The Magic of Sherwood   69
The Rainbow Gate   14
The Rapids   12
The Sea   11
The Siren   31
The Spirit Child   67
The Swimming Carnival   98
The Unforgettable Image of One Child's Pain   43
The Visitation   13
The Vultures   54
The Wild Bunch   70
The World's Greatest Gift   99
Tinkerbell   90
To Believe   59

Unsure   30
Wartime   66
What Are We To Do   64
What We've Been Through   6
Where Are You Lord?   40
Why Creation?   18